Pests, Plagues and Parasites

Mick Gowar

OXFORD

UNIVERSITY PRESS

OXFORD
UNIVERSITY PRESS

Great Clarendon Street, Oxford OX2 6DP

Oxford University Press is a department of the University of Oxford.
It furthers the University's objective of excellence in research, scholarship,
and education by publishing worldwide in

Oxford   New York

Auckland   Cape Town   Dar es Salaam   Hong Kong   Karachi
Kuala Lumpur   Madrid   Melbourne   Mexico City   Nairobi
New Delhi   Shanghai   Taipei   Toronto

With offices in

Argentina   Austria   Brazil   Chile   Czech Republic   France   Greece
Guatemala   Hungary   Italy   Japan   Poland   Portugal   Singapore
South Korea   Switzerland   Thailand   Turkey   Ukraine   Vietnam

Oxford is a registered trade mark of Oxford University Press
in the UK and in certain other countries

Text © Mick Gowar 2006

Database right Oxford University Press (maker)

First published 2006

British Library Cataloguing in Publication Data

Data available

ISBN 978-0-19-917947-3

7 9 10 8

Printed in China by Imago

Acknowledgements

The publisher would like to thank the following for permission to reproduce photographs: **p7** Science Photo
Library/Steve Gschmeissner, **p8** Science Photo Library/Sinclair Stammers, **p10t** Science Photo Library/Astrid &
Hanns-Frieder Michler, l SPL/Andrew Syred, r Adrea/Pascal Goetgheluck, **p11** NHPA/Gerry Cambridge, **p12** SPL/Eye
of Science, **p13** Alamy/Robert Slade, **p14** Alamy/Cephas Picture Library, **p15** Corbis, **p18** Bridgemand Art
Library/Biblioteque de L'Arsenal, Paris, France, Archives Charmet Dutch, **p20** Alamy/Medical-on-Line, **p21cr** Ardea,
t SPL/John Burbridge, bl Science Photo Library, r Alamy/Visual Arts Library, **p22t** Illustrated London News, **p22b**
Science Photo Library/Nigel Cattlin, **p23t** & **p25** Illustrated London News, **p26** Science Photo Library/London School
of Hygiene and Tropical Medicine, **p27c** Science Photo Library, r Science Photo Library/Martin Dohrn, **p28c**
Corbis/Bettmann, l Welcome Picture Library, **p29t** Mary Evans Picture Library, r Welcome Picture Library

Cover photograph by: Photodisc/OUP

Illlustrations by: **p4**, **p5**, **p7** Roger Gorringe, **p6** Andy Hamilton, **p8/9**, **p10**, **p11**, **p12**, **p13** Andy Parker,
p16, **p17** Daria Petrilli/Beehive Illustration

Extracts on pages 24 and 25 reprinted with kind permission of The Illustrated London News

Design by John Walker

Every effort has been made to contact copyright holders of material reproduced in this book. If notified,
the publishers will be pleased to rectify any errors or omissions at the earliest opportunity

Contents

Introduction

All living things need food. Green plants take water from the soil using their roots, take in carbon dioxide from the air and make their own food in their leaves using the power of sunlight. This is called photosynthesis – which means 'made from light'.

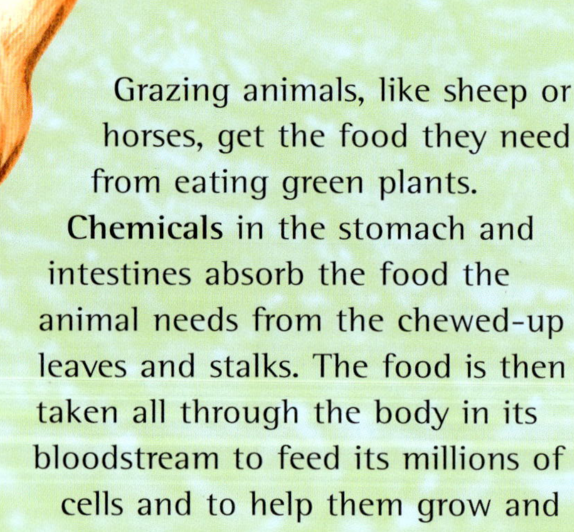

Grazing animals, like sheep or horses, get the food they need from eating green plants. **Chemicals** in the stomach and intestines absorb the food the animal needs from the chewed-up leaves and stalks. The food is then taken all through the body in its bloodstream to feed its millions of cells and to help them grow and stay healthy.

Other animals, like lions and wolves, get their food from killing and eating plant eaters. Some animals, like humans, are able to eat both meat and plants.

But parasites are animals or plants that don't hunt or graze or make their own food. They live on or inside other living things and take their food directly from their **host**.

Tiny parasitic worms can live in the bloodstream of animals and absorb their food from the host animal's blood. Ticks, lice and fleas live outside their host but feed by biting an animal and drinking its blood.

Plants also have parasites. Fungi and moulds can grow on their leaves and stems and take the food they need from their host's sap, just like an animal parasite drinking its host's blood.

This book is about parasites. Many parasites, like head lice or fleas, are a nuisance which make their host uncomfortable when they bite. Pests, like woodworm (furniture beetle), can cause household problems. There are some parasites, like certain species of mosquitoes and fleas, that can spread deadly diseases as well.

Head lice

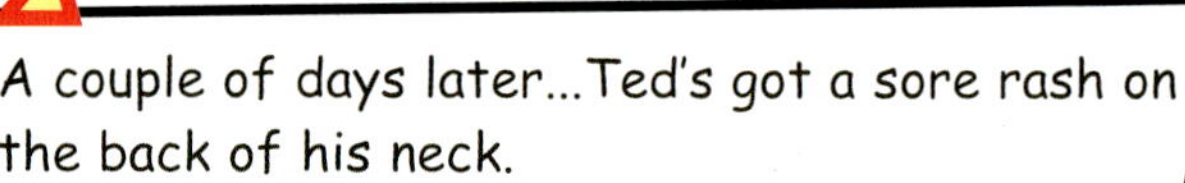

Chances are that you or someone you know has had head lice. Every year, one in ten primary school children in the United Kingdom catches head lice – that's more than half a million children!

Lousy Facts

Head lice are small insects, about the size of a sesame seed. They live by sucking human blood. They bite into the scalp, which causes the itching, and feed on the blood from the tiny blood vessels.

They only live for about 30 days, but in that time a female head louse can lay up to 100 eggs, which she glues to the shafts of hair. The eggs are known as nits. It takes 7–10 days for the eggs to hatch and another 7–10 days before the young females can start laying their own eggs.

Head lice don't have wings, so they can't fly. They don't have back legs either, so they don't jump, but they can crawl very fast using their six front legs. They can only spread through direct contact – that means they have to crawl from one person's head to another. Occasionally, they can be spread by sharing combs and hair brushes, but that's rare.

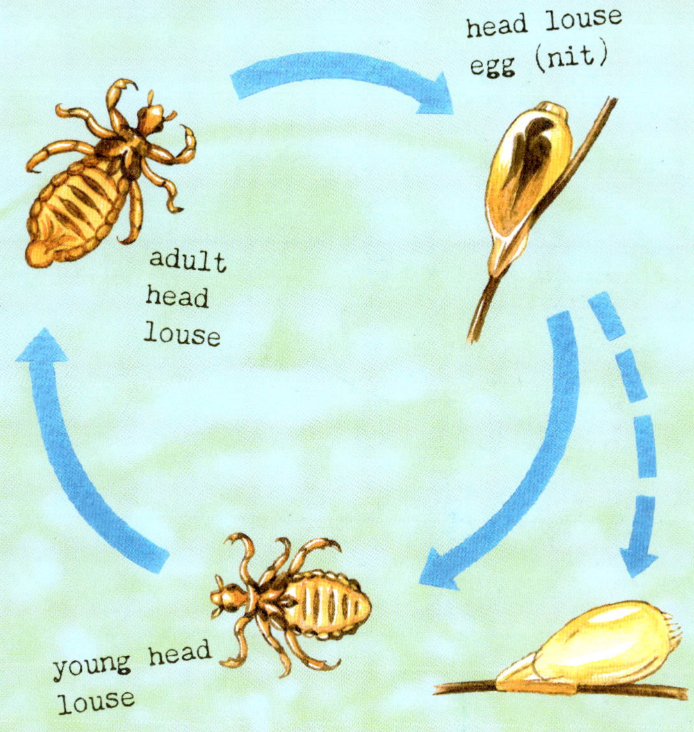

Lousy Myths

1. You can catch head lice from going swimming with someone who has them.

No, head lice can't jump, fly or swim. They have to crawl from head to head.

2. You can catch head lice from pets.

No, human blood is their only food. If they aren't on a human head, they'll die of starvation within 24 hours.

3. Only people with long, dirty hair get head lice.

No, head lice seem equally happy to live on long, short, clean or dirty hair.

Just because they're small...

There are lots of tiny parasites and pests all over your house. They can live on your pets, in your furniture and bedding, even in the wooden beams in the roof. And just because they're small, it doesn't mean they can't do a lot of harm.

Parasitic worms can live in the intestines of cats and dogs, feeding on the food our pets are **digesting**.

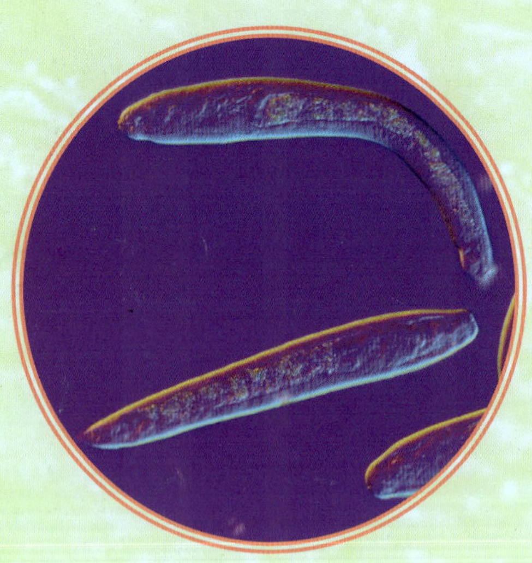

These worms live in the gut of a cat.

When a female worm lays her eggs inside the cat's gut, the eggs leave the cat's body in its droppings. The eggs can live in the soil for months or even years until another cat picks them up on its paws or coat. The eggs get into the gut when the cat licks its fur to clean it. Now they can grow into adult worms and lay their own eggs.

Living room

Lots of little holes in your dining room table or in the wooden legs of your chairs could mean you've got woodworm.

The holes are caused by the newly-hatched beetle larva hammering its way out of the wood with its head!

Adult female lays eggs.

6 weeks

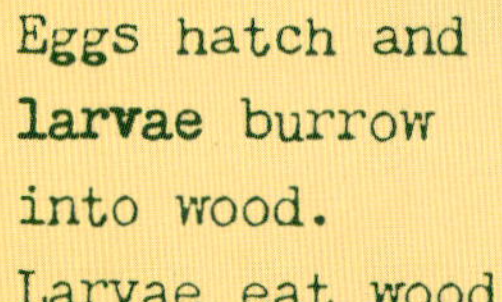

Eggs hatch and **larvae** burrow into wood. Larvae eat wood.

Adult emerges from hole.

1-5 years

2-3 weeks

Pupa form.

Beat the bug

* Paint or spray infected wood with a solution of a chemical called boron, which kills the eggs, larvae and adult beetles.

* Mend and fill any cracks in furniture or floorboards.

Bedroom 1

Clothes moths originally lived on the fur and feathers of wild animals and birds; now they feed on clothes, carpets, rugs and **upholstery** in homes.

It's not the moth that eats the clothes, it's the larvae. They especially like feeding in dark places, such as under collars and cuffs. They either spin a silken tube and feed in it, or spin a tiny mat and feed under that.

Bedroom 2

Everyone sheds around 5–10 grams of dead skin every week, and that's what dust mites eat.

Dust mites are only 0.2 millimetres long. They are virtually impossible to see without a microscope, and your mattress can contain up to 10 million mites – all eating your dead skin.

It's not the mites themselves that cause people health problems, it's something even smaller – their droppings. Mite droppings can cause asthma, **eczema** and hay fever. So if you or someone else in your family suffers from these allergies, it might be the fault of the tiny dust mites (and their even tinier droppings).

Dust mites' favourite place to live is in your mattress or pillow.

Beat the bug

* Sleep on mattresses and pillows with **synthetic** fillings.
* Put plastic covers on mattresses.
* Clean bedding and vacuum carpets regularly.

Attic

Death watch beetles are much larger than furniture beetles. The larvae can be up to 11 millimetres long, and they cause much more damage. They can eat their way through the thickest wooden beams. Death watch beetles can actually bring a house down!

They get their name from the call of the male looking for a mate, which he makes by beating his lower jaw on the side of his tunnel. People thought it sounded like the roll of drums at an execution, and if someone in the house was ill, some people believed that the sound of the death watch beetle meant they were going to die.

Parasite treasure

Truffles

Not all parasites are harmful, though. Some are highly prized.

One of the most costly foods in the world is the truffle – a **fungus** which lives on dead and

dying tree roots. Truffles are used to flavour food, such as omelettes and sauces.

Because they grow underground, truffles have to be hunted, using specially trained dogs or pigs. Both dogs and pigs have a more highly developed sense of smell than humans and can smell truffles buried several metres underground.

In France, black truffles can be sold for nearly £400 per kilogram, and in America for more than £800 per kilogram. Not surprisingly, there are stories of prize truffles being stolen, gunfights between truffle hunters, and even champion truffle hunting pigs being kidnapped!

Mistletoe

The most sacred plant of the ancient **Celtic** people was a parasite: the mistletoe. It grows on the branches and trunks of oak and apple trees and sends roots deep into the tree to drink the sap – the plant equivalent of sucking blood.

The **Druids**, the priests of the ancient Celtic peoples, believed mistletoe was an antidote against all poisons and could even raise the dead.

A Welsh Druid cutting mistletoe.

Mistletoe is used today in herbal remedies for dizziness and **epilepsy**.

The Vikings also believed that mistletoe had great powers. Turn over to read a Viking story about the mistletoe's powers, which may have started the tradition of kissing under the mistletoe.

Balder the Beautiful

Balder was the Norse god of joy, beauty and light and the son of the god-king Odin and his queen, Frigga. Everyone loved Balder, but one night Frigga had a terrible dream that Balder was killed.

She told the other gods her dream. They were horrified, because they believed that if Balder died all life on Earth would die with him. So Frigga spoke to everything on Earth and made each thing promise not to hurt Balder. She missed only one: the mistletoe that clung to the oak tree and looked just like a shoot from the tree itself.

The trickster god, Loki, was watching and saw Frigga's mistake. He planned terrible mischief.

Nothing could harm Balder, so the gods used him as the target when they practised archery. One afternoon, Hoder, the blind god, asked if he could have a turn. Everyone laughed, except Loki.

'Here,' whispered Loki, 'take this arrow and fire it at Balder.' He handed Hoder an arrow made of mistletoe.

'Here I am, brother,' called Balder. 'Don't be afraid, you can't hurt me!'

Hoder fired. The arrow plunged into Balder's heart, killing him instantly.

Frigga cursed the mistletoe. For three days and nights she tried every plant to find something that would bring Balder back to life. Nothing worked. In fury, she crushed the mistletoe's berries, and the juice fell onto Balder, who opened his eyes.

Frigga was so delighted that Balder was alive again, she lifted the curse on the berries. Frigga then kissed everyone who passed beneath the mistletoe and commanded that anyone meeting under it in future should exchange a kiss and pass on their way in peace and joy.

The Black Death (Bubonic plague)

In 1347, people living near the Black Sea port of Caffa began dying of a horrible disease. Huge boils (called buboes) appeared in their armpits and groins, they developed high fevers and died in terrible pain. Hardly anyone survived once they had caught the plague.

The plague had begun in China and spread to the Black Sea, but the local people blamed a group of Italian traders who lived in Caffa.

They raised an army and laid siege to Caffa. During the siege they used huge catapults to throw the corpses of plague victims into the city. They thought this would punish the foreigners, who they still believed were spreading the plague deliberately.

Soon, the Italian traders began to fall ill. They escaped from the town and sailed back to Italy, taking the plague with them.

Within months, the plague spread from Italy to France, Germany, Belgium, Holland, Spain and Britain. It didn't matter how rich or poor, young or old, strong or weak you were: the plague could strike you down before you even realized you had it.

Between 1347 and 1350 about 25 million people – one third of the total population of Europe – died of the plague.

And nobody knew what caused it.

Scholars in the universities said it was caused by the planets Saturn, Jupiter and Mars, which were all in a line two years before. Many doctors thought the plague was caused by bad smells and wore strange beak-like masks to protect themselves.

Many people believed the plague was a punishment from God for their sins.

Some people thought they could stop the plague by punishing themselves. They made long processions and walked from town to town lashing themselves with whips and praying aloud to show God how sorry they were.

But the Black Death wasn't caused by bad smells or by an angry God. It was caused by two parasites. The first parasite was the tiny **bacteria** in the blood of the black rat, which made the rat very ill. The second parasite was the flea. When a flea bit a sick rat and then a human, it would pass the bacteria to the human which gave them the plague.

Flea drinks rat's blood containing bacteria.

Bacteria multiply so quickly in flea's gut, flea turns black.

Flea becomes ravenously hungry and bites humans. Bacteria gets into wound and ...

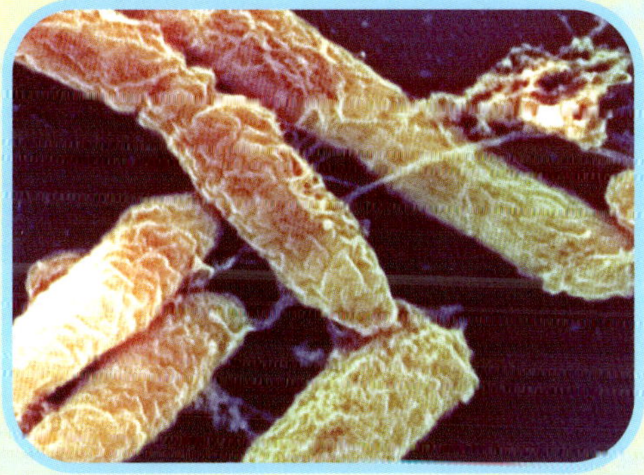

human catches the plague.

Once it was caught by a human, the disease could change into a new form which could be spread from person to person, through coughing and sneezing, like the common cold.

Today we can treat the plague with antibiotics, but in the 1350s there was no treatment. No wonder people thought it was the end of the world.

The Irish potato famine

There's an old saying, 'don't put all your eggs in one basket', meaning don't rely on just one thing. In the 19th century the peasant farmers of Ireland relied completely on potatoes. Potatoes were all they could grow on their tiny plots of land. Potatoes were the only food that fed them and their families, and selling part of their potato crop was the only way they could make money to pay the rent for the land on which they grew their potatoes. But in 1845, all over Ireland, the potato crop rotted.

At first, people blamed a fog which had recently spread across Ireland, but the real cause was a tiny fungus which fed on the leaves and **tubers** of the potato plant. The fungus had been brought to Ireland from America in the hold of a ship.

The fungus spread by minute **spores**, like tiny seeds, which could be blown in the wind from plant to plant. Just one infected plant could result in millions of spores, each of which could infect a healthy potato plant.

The people of Ireland began to starve. As the peasant farmers failed to pay their rents, many landlords threw them out of their homes. In those days the only places for homeless people to go were the workhouses. But these became full to bursting, and as the starving people crowded in, deadly diseases like cholera and typhoid started to spread.

Bread being given to starving Irish farm workers.

Some of the landlords and landowners made jobs for the starving farm workers, such as mending roads and building walls. But many were too weak from hunger to do the work. Here's part of a letter, written by a landowner, reprinted in *The Illustrated London News*:

'Buckley dropped dead on the works, after a journey of three miles before day... he had not sufficient food the night before he died... and the rest of his family lived thirty-six hours on wild weeds to spare a bit of the cake for him.... This horrifying economy is practised by scores of families in this district... I fear we must bury the dead coffinless in future. My God! what a revolting idea! Without food when alive, without a coffin when dead.'

And here's a report from a journalist who travelled across Ireland to see the suffering for himself:

'We came to Clonakilty, where the coach stopped for breakfast; and here, for the first time, the horrors of the poverty became visible, in the vast number of famished poor, who flocked around the coach to beg alms: amongst them was a woman carrying in her arms the corpse of a fine child, and making the most distressing appeal to the passengers for aid to enable her to purchase a coffin and bury her dear little baby... I learned from the people of the hotel that each day brings dozens of such applicants into the town.'

One million people died of starvation or disease, and two million left Ireland to find work and food in England or America. This was all caused by the minute spores of a tiny parasite that fed on the potato plants.

Malaria

Malaria parasites
in human blood

Every year, 800,000 babies and children in Africa die from malaria. That means that in the time it's taken you to read this far on the page, two African children have died from malaria. Across the world every year, 500 million suffer from malaria, and between one and one-and-a-half million people die from the disease.

Malaria is passed from person to person by mosquitoes which bite infected people, pick up the tiny parasites from their blood while feeding, and then inject them into the next person they feed on: similar to the way the Black Death spread in Europe.

The parasites live and multiply in the liver, brain and blood cells. They cause fevers, shivering and, in the worst cases, coma and death.

Malaria has been killing people for hundreds of thousands
– maybe even millions – of years, but it's only in the last
100 years that scientists have understood how the disease
is spread. We still don't have a cure, but if you turn to the
next page you can find out about the race to find one.

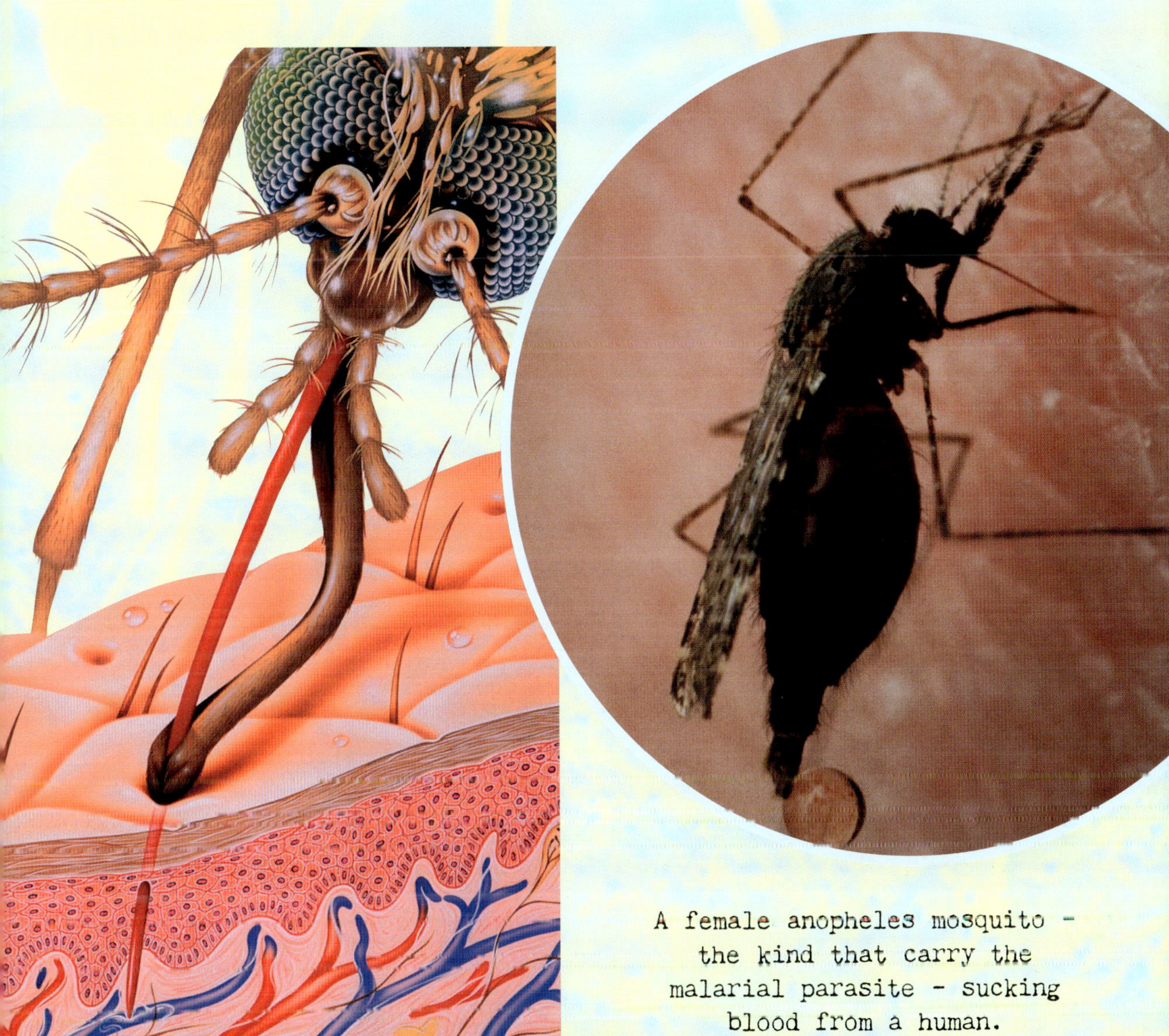

A female anopheles mosquito –
the kind that carry the
malarial parasite – sucking
blood from a human.

6,000 BC First written mention of malaria on a clay tablet found in Iraq

500 BC Ancient Greek doctor Hippocrates writes about three types of malaria

2005 – Present World still waiting for effective malaria vaccine

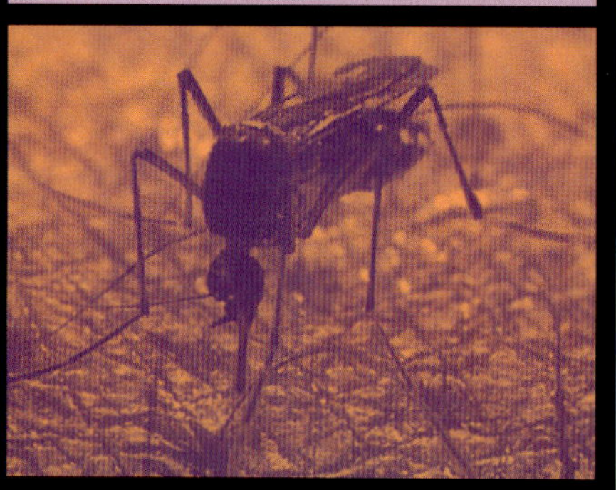

1992 Tests begin on the first possible **vaccine** for one type of malaria

THE

1966 'New' drug Qinghaosu is developed from sweet wormwood. (The wormwood plant has been used in China to treat malaria for 2,000 years)

1956–72 The World Health Organisation starts a campaign to completely destroy malaria. US$1 billion is spent on spraying houses with DDT and draining swamps. The campaign fails

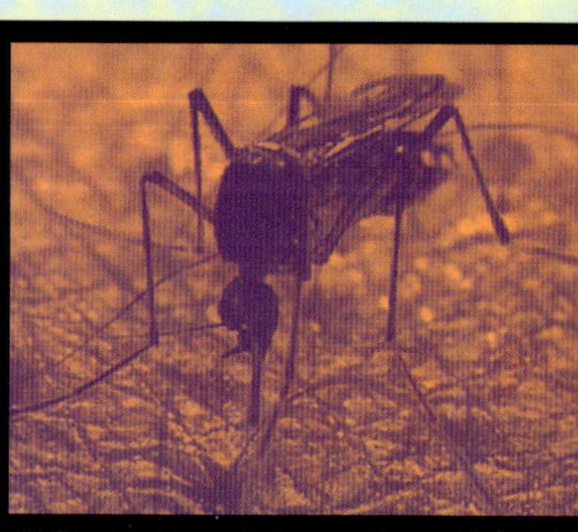

1640 Huan del Vego, one of the European explorers in South America, learns from Peruvian Indians how to use the bark of the cinchona tree to treat malaria

1770 An Italian scientist called Giovanni Lancisi suggests that malaria is caused by the bad air from swamps and names the disease 'malaria' – the Italian for bad air

1829 Two French chemists, Pierre-Joseph Pelletier and Joseph-Bienamie Caventou, extract quinine from cinchona bark. Quinine is still one of the main drugs for treating malaria

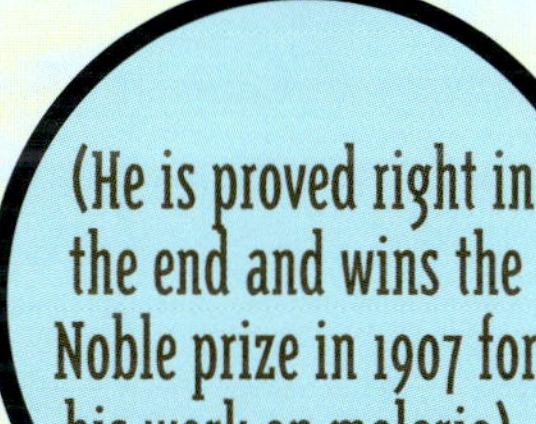

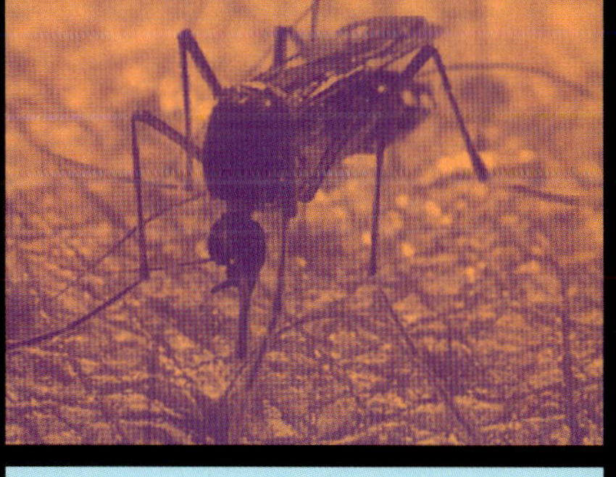

1880 Alphonse Laveran, a French doctor working in Algeria, sees the malaria parasite while looking at slides of blood samples under the microscope. Other doctors and scientists don't believe him

1939 A new insecticide, DDT, is proved to kill malaria-carrying mosquitoes. Spraying with DDT becomes a common practice in treating malaria

1930–40 New anti-malaria drug, chloroquine, is developed which is much safer and cheaper than quinine

1887 Ronald Ross, a British Army surgeon, proves that the anopheline mosquito is the way malaria spreads

Glossary

bacteria – simple, one-celled creatures that live in water, soil or on and in the bodies of animals and plants. Many are parasites. Bacteria are often thought to cause diseases, but only a small number of species do

Celt – a race of people who lived in Europe before the Roman conquests. They are the ancestors of modern Welsh, Cornish and Breton people

chemical - a substance which is used to make or help a chemical reaction. We use chemicals to cause chemical reactions every day, for example detergents which can break down oil and grease can be used in washing-up liquids, or salt which can raise the melting point of ice is often spread on the roads in winter to get rid of ice and snow

digest - break down foods in the stomach and intestines so the body can absorb them easily

Druid –a priest of the ancient Celtic religion

eczema – red itchy patches of dried skin, often on the inside of elbows and knees. Eczema cannot be passed from one person to another, but like hay fever and asthma it can be caused by an allergic reaction to things like dust mite droppings

epilepsy - a disorder caused by the interruption of electrical signals in the brain. In mild cases this can mean losing consciousness for just a second or two, like dozing off and waking up almost immediately. In more extreme cases suffers can have fits and lose consciousness for several minutes

fungus – a plant which does not make its own food through photosynthesis, but absorbs nutrition from the dead or living plants on which it grows

host – an animal or plant which provides food for a parasite

larva – juvenile form of insect, for example, the caterpillar of a butterfly or moth

pupa – when a larva is fully grown it becomes encased in a hard coating. This is known as a pupa. While the insect is a pupa, all the cells reassemble to form the adult which often looks nothing like the larva or caterpillar

scholar – an old-fashioned word for a student, or teacher, at a university or college. Often used nowadays for a prize-winning student – the winner of a scholarship – or a student with special privileges

spore – a tiny one-celled 'seed' and the method by which fungi and similar non-flowering plants spread

synthetic – a man-made or artificial version of a natural or organic product, for example, rayon which looks like silk, but is made from oil, or saccharine which is often used as a sweetener instead of sugar

tuber – a swollen root which acts as a food store for a plant. Best known examples are potato and dahlia

upholstery – the soft, cushioned part of furniture, for example, the arms and seats of chairs or sofas

vaccine – a medicine, usually injected, which helps prevent a disease in people or animals by stimulating the body to produce antibodies – chemicals which fight particular diseases

Index